5796 8751

P9-DFV-019

IN MY BACKYARD

frogs

by Lindsy J. O'Brien

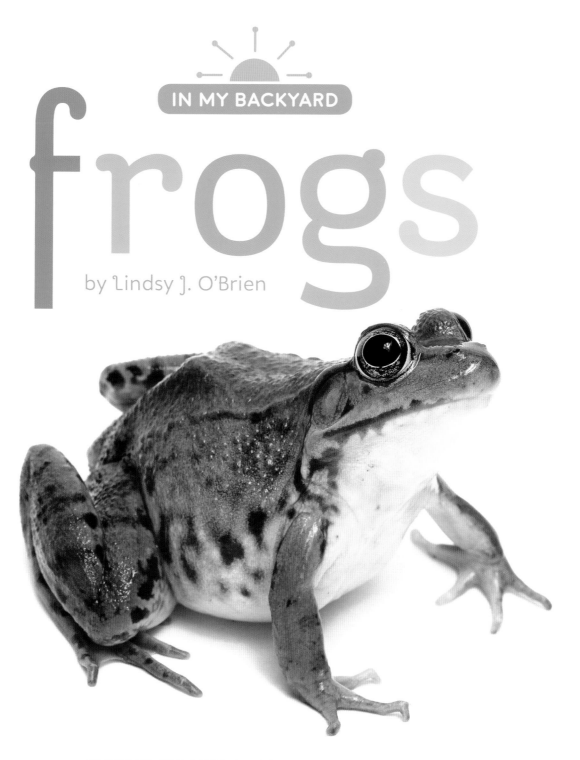

CREATIVE EDUCATION • CREATIVE PAPERBACKS

Published by Creative Education and Creative Paperbacks
P.O. Box 227, Mankato, Minnesota 56002
Creative Education and Creative Paperbacks are imprints of
The Creative Company
www.thecreativecompany.us

Design and production by Chelsey Luther
Art direction by Rita Marshall
Printed in China

Photographs by Alamy (Danita Delimont, Christina Rollo,
ZUMA Press), Corbis (Michael Durham/Minden Pictures, Gallo
Images), Dreamstime (Michiel De Wit, Eastmanphoto, Dirk
Ercken, Adam Gryko, Isselee, Sdbower), Getty Images (Gary
Mezaros/Visuals Unlimited, Inc.), iStockphoto (Antagain,
GlobalP), Shutterstock (IrinaK, Eric Isselee, Mirek Kijewski, Vibe
Images), SuperStock (Flirt/Flirt, Thomas Marent/ardea.com/
Pant/Pantheon, Minden Pictures/Minden Pictures)

Library of Congress Cataloging-in-Publication Data
O'Brien, Lindsy J.
Frogs / by Lindsy J. O'Brien.
p. cm. — (In my backyard)
Includes bibliographical references and index.
Summary: A high-interest introduction to the life cycle of
frogs, including how tadpoles develop, their insect diet,
threats from predators, and the wet habitats of these
backyard animals.

ISBN 978-1-60818-698-3 (hardcover)
ISBN 978-1-62832-294-1 (pbk)
ISBN 978-1-56660-734-9 (eBook)
1. Frogs—Juvenile literature.

QL668.E2 O235 2016
597.8/9—dc23   2015034524

CCSS: RI.1.1, 2, 3, 4, 5, 6, 7; RI.2.1, 2, 4, 5, 6, 7, 10; RF.1.1, 3, 4;
RF.2.3, 4

First Edition HC 9 8 7 6 5 4 3 2 1
First Edition PBK 9 8 7 6 5 4 3 2 1

Contents

The grass moves in front of you. You see something small and greenish brown. It is a frog! Frogs are amphibians. They live on land and in water.

Most frogs lay eggs that hatch into tadpoles. Tadpoles have large heads. A tail helps the tadpole swim. Then it grows legs. It becomes an adult frog.

egg

tadpole

froglet

Frogs' eggs will hatch faster if they are laid in warm water.

id you know there are more than 4,000 types of frogs? Many frogs are green or brown. Poison dart frogs are more colorful. Female frogs are usually bigger than males. Their bodies have to store the eggs.

poison dart frog

leopard frog

Some frog sounds can be heard from as far as a mile (1.6 km) away.

Frogs live in lakes and wetlands. You might even find them in trees! In places that have cold winters, frogs hibernate. They bury themselves in mud. They find hiding spots on land.

Frogs do not have to drink water because their skin takes it into the body.

unting frogs catch food with their tongues. The tongues snap out and curl around prey. Frogs eat insects, minnows, and spiders. Sometimes they eat worms! Would you like to share a meal with a frog?

Frogs do not chew often but swallow their prey in one piece.

13

Some frogs are as tiny as a coin. Others can grow as large as footballs! Most frogs have skin between their toes. This is called webbing. Webbed feet help frogs swim.

Tree frogs (right) have toe pads, not webbed feet, to grip things.

Frogs have strong jumping legs. Jumping and swimming help frogs escape from predators. Fish, birds, and snakes all like to eat frogs.

Many frogs can jump more than 20 times their body length.

You can find frogs almost everywhere! Look around you. Watch for movement in the grass or water. Will you find a frog next time you are outside?

Pacific tree frogs (right) usually lay eggs on or beneath flower petals.

Frogs come in many different colors. Those colors match the world around them. This helps the frogs hide from predators. It also helps them sneak up on prey.

Materials you need: pencil, crayons or markers, and paper

Green Frog

Hide the Frog

1. With a pencil, draw lines to create three sections on your page.

2. Draw a frog in each section.

3. Imagine your frogs are colored to match the world around them. In the first section, color your frog to make it hide in fall leaves.

4. In the second section, color your frog to make it hide in bright flowers.

5. In the last section, color your frog to make it hide up in a tree.

If you have time, draw and color each frog's habitat. Show your drawing to your friends. Can they find your frogs?

Glossary

amphibians: cold-blooded animals that can live on land and in fresh water

hibernate: to spend the winter sleeping or not moving around much

predators: animals that hunt other animals for food

prey: animals that are hunted and eaten by other animals

tadpoles: the swimming, tailed young of amphibians that breathe through openings in the skin called gills

Read More

Carney, Elizabeth. *Frogs!*
Washington, D.C.: National Geographic, 2009.

Marent, Thomas, and Tom Jackson. *Frog.*
New York: DK Publishing, 2008.

Websites

Easy Science for Kids: All About Frogs and Toads
http://easyscienceforkids.com/all-about-frogs-and-toads/
Learn how to tell frogs and toads apart.

National Wildlife Federation: Observe Frogs
http://www.nwf.org/kids/family-fun/outdoor-activities
/observing-frogs.aspx
Explore nature with Ranger Rick and learn more about
frogs!

Note: Every effort has been made to ensure that the websites listed above are suitable for
children, that they have educational value, and that they contain no inappropriate mate-
rial. However, because of the nature of the Internet, it is impossible to guarantee that these
sites will remain active indefinitely or that their contents will not be altered.

Index